BAZOOKA BOYS!

Be Strong & Be Brave...
for the Lord your God is with you.

Deuteronomy 31:6

By
Kristie Kerr & Paula Yarnes
with
Jeff Kerr & Aaron Broberg

Copyright 2014 Kristie Kerr and Paula Yarnes. All Rights Reserved.

No part of this book may be reproduced, transmitted, or utilized in any form or by any means, graphic, electronic or mechanical, including photocopying, recording, taping, or by any information storage or retrieval, without the permission in writing from the publisher.

Unless otherwise indicated, all Scripture quotations are taken from the Holy Bible, New Living Translation, copyright ©1996, 2004, 2007 by Tyndale House Foundation. Used by permission of Tyndale House Publishers, Inc., Carol Stream, Illinois 60188. All rights reserved.

THE HOLY BIBLE, NEW INTERNATIONAL VERSION®, NIV® Copyright © 1973, 1978, 1984, 2011 by Biblica, Inc.™ Used by permission. All rights reserved worldwide.

Scripture taken from The Message. Copyright ©1993, 1994, 1995, 1996, 2000, 2001, 2002. Used by permission of NavPress Publishing Group.

Scripture taken from the Contemporary English Version ©1991, 1992, 1995 by American Bible Society, Used by Permission.

Scripture taken from the Common English Bible P.O. Box 801 201 Eighth Avenue South Nashville, TN 37202-0801

Scripture taken from the International Standard Version Release 2.1. Copyright ©1996–2012 the ISV Foundation. All rights reserved internationally.

ISBN: 978-0-9840312-7-6

Printed in the United States of America

1st Printing

CONTENTS

How to Use This Book vii

Getting to Know Him 1-23
    Large Group Lesson 2
    Bible Blitz 11
    Bazooka Project 13
    Team Huddle 15
    Parent Connection 16
    Doodle Page 17
    Take Home Activity Pages
        Kindergarten – 1st Grade 19
        2nd – 3rd Grade 21
        4th – 5th Grade 23

God the Father 25-49
    Large Group Lesson 26
    Bible Blitz 35
    Bazooka Project 37
    Team Huddle 39
    Parent Connection 40
    Doodle Page 41
    Take Home Activity Pages
        Kindergarten – 1st Grade 43
        2nd – 3rd Grade 45
        4th – 5th Grade 47

God the Son (Jesus) 51-69
    Large Group Lesson 52
    Bible Blitz 57
    Bazooka Project 59
    Team Huddle 61
    Parent Connection 62
    Doodle Page 63
    Take Home Activity Pages
        Kindergarten – 1st Grade 65
        2nd – 3rd Grade 67
        4th – 5th Grade 69

God the Holy Spirit 73-93
    Large Group Lesson 74
    Bible Blitz 81
    Bazooka Project 83
    Team Huddle 85
    Parent Connection 86
    Doodle Page 87
    Take Home Activity Pages
        Kindergarten – 1st Grade 89
        2nd – 3rd Grade 91
        4th – 5th Grade 93

Bazooka Bash 95-100

Dedicated to the boys who inspire us:

To Charlie whose tender heart and quiet spirit
remind us that **STRENGTH ISN'T ALWAYS LOUD**.

To Hunter who is **TENACIOUS AND KIND**…
and came up with the name Bazooka Boys.

To Chase who **LOVES UNCONDITIONALLY**.

To Reed who lit his homework on fire…
and then became an **HONOR STUDENT**.

To Jacob, the boy with the sensitive heart,
that captures people with his **LOVE FOR JUSTICE AND ALL THINGS SILLY**.

To Levi whose **DETERMINATION COULD DEMOLISH MOUNTAINS**
& smile could melt away the debris

To Zach who is a **TRUSTWORTHY, CONFIDENT, KIND-HEARTED** young man,
and NEVER forgets to kiss his mom goodnight!

To Li who is **KIND AND LOVING** and ALWAYS follows the rules!

To Stewart. The **TWINKLE IN YOUR EYE** and the tenderness in your heart
remind us that God really does make dreams come true.

You amaze us.
Go change the world.

Bazooka Boys ★ Knowing God

HOW TO USE THIS BOOK

It seems easy enough, right? Like you really shouldn't need a page just to tell you how to use this book. And yet, here we are. We are nothing if we're not efficient!

Ok. This resource was written as a tool for use in a large group, small group or even for your family. Obviously, your specific needs may vary according to the size and make up of your group, but we have hopefully provided you with enough options that you have plenty of... well, options.

One component that we hope will help you immensely is our "Bazooka Blast Overview" located at the beginning of each chapter. This is a one page synopsis of each week's lesson. Our male co-authors have assured us that male leaders prefer fewer words than our Polka Dot Girls leaders (huh... who knew?)... so we've given you the option of "just the facts."

Each chapter starts with a large group lesson. This is something that can be taught by one teacher or even a variety of leaders. These lessons are designed to appeal to all age groups – so bring all your boys together for this part of the night. There are illustrations provided, but feel free to add in your own thoughts, insights and stories! The boys will love to hear about your own personal experiences and perspective.

*Note: if you don't have enough space or leaders to divide your boys and girls, the Polka Dot Girls and Bazooka Boys large group lessons can be taught together. The main points of the large group lesson are usually the same – and can be adapted to teach both genders. Then consider breaking up the boys and girls into gender specific groups for small group and activity time or simply provide the Polka Dot Girls activities for the girls and the Bazooka Boys activities for the boys!

Following the large group time, we have put together a section called Bazooka Blitz which includes fun activites and games to reinforce what was learned in the lesson. We know that boys learn best while actively engaged, so we've created elements that combine scripture exploration with fun games. Boys love competition. They want to know who is the strongest, fastest and smartest. Use competition to encourage participation in small group discussion & activities. There should always be a winner. Boys won't want to participate in a competition if no one wins. Life is full of successes and failures and learning how to handle them is an important life skill.

Then it's project time! We know that some groups like to do a long term project such as creating Pinewood Derby cars – but if you want something different, we've included boy-approved and "as masculine as we can possibly make a craft" activities. Make sure you do adequate preparation depending on the age and skill level of your boys. Nothing is more frustrating than running out of time because you spent too much time cutting things out or waiting for glue to dry. (By the way… glue dries REALLY slow. Even slower when you want it to dry fast. Just our experience anyway….)

After your project time, it's time for our favorite part of the night: Team Huddle Time. This is a time to have some discussion and connection with the boys.

Huddle Time is broken down like this:

Ask This: Discussion Questions

Within each lesson you will find 3 discussion questions. We've made them short and sweet. Encourage the boys to share their stories and help them draw parallels between the spiritual truths they've learned this week and their everyday-real life situations.

Repeat This: Bible Review

Have the boys repeat the theme verse for the week. Try repeating it a few times or even let them practice individually. And we would not be opposed to some sort of "sugary reward" for those who learn it. Anything to get them to learn God's Word!

Pray This: Prayer Time

This is a great time to find out what's going on in the boy's lives. Take prayer requests and spend time praying for their needs. Challenge the boys to pray for one another and then follow up next week and see how God has answered their prayers.

Doodle This: Journal Time

Use the "Doddle This" template page (or find the corresponding page in the workbooks if the boys have purchased them separately) to have the boys explore the topics in a more personal way. Many boys are not highly verbal. They may communicate or learn better by drawing. If you don't have time, feel free to send it home and encourage them to spend some time working on it during the week.

Lastly, we've included some pages to be photocopied and sent home. They include age appropriate activity sheets and a parent partner. These are intended to give the boys some fun tools to work on throughout the week and to let the parents see what their sons are learning.

And the MOST important thing to remember is to MAKE IT WORK FOR YOU. Every group is unique and different, so feel free to add, subtract, edit, rewrite, and rework anything you find here. Find out what works and stick with it and don't be afraid to chuck the stuff that isn't working.

Our job is simple – but it couldn't be more important. We get the amazing privilege of teaching these boys about Jesus. We pray the material gives you practical tools to do just that. But above and beyond all that, remember that your gift of time and interest in these boys' lives will impact them far greater than any lesson or illustration. You are literally demonstrating for them what it means to be a man who loves Jesus. Be patient. Be loving. Be strong. Be fun. Be there.

We wish you all the best as you teach your boys what it means to be a Bazooka Boy!

BAZOOKA BLAST OVERVIEW: WEEK 1

Large Group Lesson: *(15 minutes)*
- God knows everything about you, and He wants you to know everything about him.
- Three ways we can learn more about God:
    1. Read the Bible (Psalm 119:11)
    2. Talk to God (Jeremiah 33:3)
    3. Go to church
- Summary: You can know God. You can learn about Him. You can talk to Him. He wants to be your best friend.

Bazooka Blitz: Small Group Time:

Bible Blitz *(15 minutes)*
Bible Verse Grid Toss *(Instructions on page 11)*

Bazooka Project *(20 minutes)*
Rock Necklace or Pet "God" Rocks *(Instructions on page 13)*

Team Huddle *(10 minutes)*

<u>Ask This:</u>
1. In one word, describe what is unique about you.
2. How could you get to know God better?
   Possible Answers: Read the Bible, Pray, Go to church
3. Name 1 cool thing about God.
   Possible Answers: He created everything, He's super strong, He knows everything

<u>Repeat This:</u> Psalm 145:8

<u>Pray This:</u> *"God, thanks for knowing everything about me. I want to know everything about You. Show me something I don't know about You this week."*

<u>Doodle This:</u> *(Follow Doodle page instructions)*

<u>Take Home:</u> Doodle pages, activity sheets and parent connection.

Bazooka Boys ★ Knowing God

GETTING TO KNOW HIM

What's the Point?
God knows everything about you,
and He wants you to know everything about Him.

THEME VERSE:
The Lord is close to all who call on Him.
Psalm 145:18

RELATED BIBLE PASSAGE:
Exodus 4:1–17

★ LARGE GROUP LESSON ★
(15 minutes)

Caleb was six years old when he met Jacob. It had been raining for a few days, and the baseball fields by his house had flooded and turned into one giant mud pit. Caleb stood along the side of the field, wondering if he should jump in. Suddenly, he saw Jacob standing on the other side of the field, sizing up the situation. They caught each others eye, gave each other a nod, and both jumped headfirst into the gooey black mud.

They've been best friends ever since.

Having a good friend is a super cool thing. You can ride your bikes together, play catch, and hang out playing your favorite video game. A good friend is someone you know you can count on, someone who has your back and will always stand beside you. It's cool to know that there is someone you know will be there for you.

And you know what? God wants to be a friend like that.

Bazooka Boys ★ Knowing God

Sometimes it can seem like God is great big and far away. It can feel like He is just way too big to care about you. But the truth is, God wants to be your friend!

Isn't that crazy? The great big God who made the entire universe wants to be friends with you. Psalm 25:10 says, *"O Lord, You are the friend of Your worshippers . . ."* (CEV).

God already knows everything about you. He knows what you're thinking, what you're feeling, what you're going to do today, and even what you're going to do tomorrow! The Bible tells us He even knows how many hairs you have on your head!

> "...BUT THE PEOPLE WHO KNOW THEIR GOD WILL BE STRONG AND TAKE ACTION."
> —DANIEL 11:32

I Peter 1:2 says, *"God the Father knew you and chose you long ago."* Not only does He know everything about you, but He **CHOSE** you to be His friend! Imagine the coolest, strongest, smartest, most amazing person in the world deciding that, out of all the people in the entire universe, He wants to be friends with you. That's pretty amazing!

God knows you. God loves you. And God wants you to know Him too.

So, how do you get to know God better? The same way Caleb got to know Jacob better—by spending time with him. And the more time Caleb spent with Jacob, the more he discovered the things that were important to him.

It's the same way with God.

GOD KNOWS EVERYTHING ABOUT YOU, AND HE WANTS YOU TO KNOW EVERYTHING ABOUT HIM.

There are three ways we can get to know God better.

 # 1. READING THE BIBLE

The Bible is a letter from God to you! God has lots of things that He wants to say to you. He wants to tell you about Himself. He wants to tell you about things He has done for other people. He wants to give you instructions for living your life in a way that will make Him happy.

So He gave us the Bible. He told some people, many years ago, to write down some very powerful stories and words that would help you and me understand Him better. Now, you and I can read the Bible and learn what God is like!

You can read the stories and see how God helped people. You can see how He told them to live. You can learn about His heart and how He thinks and most importantly, how much He loves you.

Travis was facing something difficult and he didn't know what to do. He had to get up in front of his whole class to give a book report. He was scared to death of talking in front of people. His knees would shake and his hands would get sweaty and he'd feel like he was going to puke. What was he going to do?

One day he opened his Bible and found a story about a man named Moses. God asked Moses to lead His people out of a really bad situation. He was to go before the Pharoah, who was the King of Egypt, and tell him to free God's people from slavery. Moses was scared! He did not want to

stand in front of the King. I can imagine that his knees were shaking and his hands were sweaty and he wanted to puke—just like Travis.

But here's what God said to Moses: *"When you speak, I will be with you and give you the words to say"* (Exodus 4:12, CEV).

Whoa! That's exactly what Travis needed to hear. It was so cool that the words God had said to Moses in the Bible could be so helpful to Travis now. He wrote the words on a little card and carried it with him on the days before he had to give his speech. When the day finally came, he read the card one more time, took a deep breath, and got up in front of the class confident that God was with him and would help him do his very best.

The Bible is full of stories just like this one that can help us get through the tough things we face in our lives. It has all kinds of wisdom and special help for us.

God uses the Bible to speak to us, but it also tells us what God is like. We learn that He is strong and He will protect us. Proverbs 18:10 says, *"The name of the Lord is a strong fortress; the godly run to him and are safe."* We can know, by reading the Bible, that God is not only powerful, but that He will protect us.

> "I HAVE HIDDEN YOUR WORD IN MY HEART, THAT I MIGHT NOT SIN AGAINST YOU."
> —PSALM 119:11

We learn that God is perfect. He never makes mistakes. He never changes. We can know that He will love us the same today as He did yesterday and will love us just as much tomorrow.

The Bible is God's adventure map for you. It's important that you read it every day so that you can learn more and more what God is like and what He wants you to do.

The second way we can know God better is by:

 ## 2. TALKING TO GOD

When Caleb and Jacob were walking home from their mud pit adventure, they couldn't stop talking about how awesome it was. Caleb said, "That was so cool when you slid through the mud into home plate!" Jacob replied, "Oh yeah . . . or when you tackled me that one time? I can't believe how muddy we are!"

They went back and forth, recounting their awesome day while the mud dripped off their shirts and shoes.

Not only did they have fun acting like crazy people in the mud, but every time they remembered what they had done and talked about it, they became closer friends. With every new adventure they had came new stories and new memories that bound them together as best buds.

> "ASK ME, AND I WILL TELL YOU REMARKABLE SECRETS . . ."
> —JEREMIAH 33:3

God wants us to talk to Him just like we talk to our friends. Actually, praying to God is really just talking to Him. He wants you to talk to Him about the things that are bothering you, the things you're excited about, and the things you're thankful for. He loves it when you share your life with Him.

Something cool happens when you talk to God. You'll begin to feel closer to Him just like you do when you are talking to your friends! It's so awesome to know He cares about the things you care about. He is always listening, and He's the best friend you could ever have.

Not only can you talk to God, He will talk to you too! Jeremiah 33:3 says, *"Ask me, and I will tell you remarkable secrets . . ."*. You may not hear His voice out

loud like you hear your mom or dad, but God will speak to your heart. I always try to write down (or even draw a picture of) the words I feel God is speaking to me so I can remember what He is saying to me. And when God speaks to you, it will always line up with what the Bible says.

If you will listen, God will speak to you. He'll give you answers to your problems. He'll challenge you to improve your attitude or behavior. He'll make you feel better when you're sad or frustrated. He'll talk to you about your future.

When God appeared to Moses and told him to lead his people out of slavery, I'm sure Moses was totally freaked out. But I think it's pretty cool that God talked to Moses. He not only gave Moses direction and instructions, but He said things to Moses that gave him courage even though he was afraid.

God is talking to you all the time. Now, it may not be in a voice you can hear, but God will speak to you. When I hear God talking to me, its like I hear the words inside my head, and I know they aren't my own thoughts. You can talk to God, and He will talk to you too!

And the last way we can grow closer to God is to:

 **3. GO TO CHURCH**

Have you ever been on a team or in a club? It's pretty cool to spend time with kids who are interested in the same things you are. You can learn from each other, help each other get better at the stuff you care about, and support each other when you go through hard times.

Church is a place where you can discover more about God and spend time with people who love Him just like you do. You'll hear stories about the things He's done in the past. You'll learn about what's in the Bible, what makes God happy, and what He doesn't want you to do. And you'll make lots of great friends and have a lot of fun too!

It's important to read your Bible and talk to God when you are at home, but something really amazing happens when you hang out with other people who believe in God like you do. It helps you grow stronger in your faith. You can talk to your teachers and your friends about God. You can ask questions about the things you're unsure about. You can have people pray for you and your family.

Illustration: Have something heavy on the stage, like a big rock. Have one boy come up and try and lift it by himself. It will be too heavy for him to carry on his own. Then have a few other boys help him lift the object.

Conclusion: Sometimes we need others to help us. We can't do it on our own, and we need the help of our friends to support us, help us, and pray for us.

Make sure that you come to church often. It's important to spend time with other people who believe in God like you do!

Summary: You can know God. You can learn about Him. You can talk to Him. He wants to be your best friend.

Bazooka Boys ★ Knowing God

GOD KNOWS EVERYTHING ABOUT YOU, AND HE WANTS YOU TO KNOW EVERYTHING ABOUT HIM.

Closing Prayer: Dear God, thank You that You know me. Thank You that you want to be my friend and that you have lots of adventures planned for my life. I want to know more about you too. Help me to spend time reading the Bible, talking to You, and learning more about You at church. Thank You for choosing me to be your friend. Amen.

Bazooka Boys ★ Knowing God

BIBLE VERSE GRID TOSS

(15 minutes)

Supplies:

- Paper
- Pen
- Bible references
- Bibles
- Bean bags (hacky sacks or a sock full of dry beans work well)
- Masking tape
- Scorecard

Directions

Write each of the following Bible references on separate sheets of paper (you can add more if you like).

- Psalm 25:10
- 1 Peter 1:2
- Psalm 119:11
- Jeremiah 33:3
- Psalm 27:8
- Exodus 4:12
- Psalm 145:18

1. Lay the sheets of paper on the floor in a grid pattern with the Bible verses face up.

2. Use the masking tape to create a designated tossing line a set distance away from the grid.

3. Split the boys into two teams (team names are always fun) and have one boy from each team stand at the tossing line with a bean bag.

4. On your mark, have each team member throw their bean bag at the grid of Scripture verses.

5. Once the bags land, each boy should grab the piece paper their bean bag fell on and bring it back to their team. If their bean bag doesn't land on a paper, they must throw it again.

6. The first team to look up the Bible verse gets the points. (Each Bible verse may have a different point value. This will add an extra layer of competition for older boys.)

7. Repeat the process until you have a winning team.

Bazooka Boys ★ Knowing God

BAZOOKA PROJECT

WEEK 1

OPTION 1: ROCK NECKLACE
(20 minutes)

<u>Supplies</u>

- Small rock for each boy
- 22 Gauge colored wire (15 inches for each boy)
- Leather cord (enough to make a necklace for each boy)
- Needle-nose pliers
- Scissors

<u>Directions</u>

- Place a rock at the center of a 15-inch-long piece of colored wire.
- Wrap the wire around the rock a few times to secure it and twist the ends together.
- Wrap the twist around a pencil to make a loop.
- Use needle-nose pliers to close the loop, then cut off any excess wire.
- Hang the pendant from a length of leather cord to make a necklace.

OPTION 2: PET "GOD" ROCKS
(20 minutes)

<u>Supplies</u>

- Rocks
- Sharpie markers
- Paint (optional)
- Google eyes (optional)
- Glue or glue dots (optional)

<u>Directions</u>

1. Decorate the rocks

2. Write one of the Scripture references on the back of the rock.
    - Psalm 25:10
    - 1 Peter 1:2
    - Psalm 119:11
    - Jeremiah 33:3
    - Psalm 27:8
    - Exodus 4:12
    - Psalm 145:18

ASK THIS ★ REPEAT THIS ★ PRAY THIS ★ DOODLE THIS
(10 minutes)

Huddle up with your team just before you dismiss.

Ask This:

1. In one word, describe what is unique about you.

2. How could you get to know God better? (Possible answers: Read the Bible, Pray, Go to church)

3. Name 1 cool thing about God. (Possible answers: He created everything, He's super strong, He knows everything)

Repeat This:

"The Lord is close to all who call on Him." –Psalm 145:18

Pray This:

"God, thanks for knowing everything about me. I want to know everything about You. Show me something I don't know about You this week."

Doodle This (optional):

Copy the Doodle page for the boys (or have them turn to that page in their workbook).

PARENT CONNECTION

This week in Bazooka Boys, we talked about knowing God. We discussed the fact that God knows everything about us, and He wants us to know everything about Him. We can be close to Him and come to Him with everything we're facing. We challenged the boys to grow closer to God by reading the Bible, talking to God, and going to church.

You can reinforce these ideas with your son by helping him grown in these three areas. Take time to pray with him before bed and let him take a turn saying the prayer. Have him think back on things he did that day and thank God for them. Also have him remember the things he struggled with or was fearful of and ask God to help him face those things with bravery and courage. It's important for him to learn to trust God and come to Him with everything he is going through.

You can also help your son look up verses in the Bible. Maybe he is struggling with fear. Get a good concordance or even look online for verses that will help him. Write the verses out and help your son remember the promises God has given him when he is feeling fearful.

Lastly, be faithful in bringing your son to Bazooka Boys and other church services and events. The amount of activities kids are involved in these days can be overwhelming, and sometimes the LAST thing you want to do is drive them one more place, but it is so important for them to learn to prioritize learning about God and being around people who can help build up their faith. These are critical days, and the more you can equip your children with knowledge of who God is, the better. You will be sending them out into the world with a toolbox full of lessons and preparation to live a life pleasing to the Lord.

Bazooka Boys ★ Knowing God

DOODLE PAGE

GOD KNOWS EVERYTHING ABOUT YOU AND HE WANTS YOU TO KNOW EVERYTHING ABOUT HIM!

Draw a picture of yourself under the "you" bubble. Then write something you would like to know more about God. Under the "God" bubble, write a cool memory about something cool that happened to you.

GOD:
I KNOW EVERYTHING ABOUT YOU. REMEMBER THE TIME WHEN WE...

YOU:
SOMETHING I WANT TO LEARN ABOUT GOD IS...

Bazooka Boys ★ Knowing God

KINDERGARTEN AND 1ST GRADE

God wants to be your very best friend! The verses below talk about knowing God. Write the word KNOW in the blank spaces.

Psalm 9:10 – *"Those who _____ your name trust in you."*

Psalm 119:168 – *"Yes, I obey your commandments and laws because you _____ everything I do."*

Psalm 139:23 – *"Search me, O God, and _____ my heart."*

Daniel 11:32 – *"But the people who _____ their God will be strong and will resist him."*

Philippians 3:10 – *"I want to _____ Christ and experience the mighty power that raised him from the dead."*

Colossians 1:10 – *"You will grow as you learn to _____ God better and better."*

Bazooka Boys ★ Knowing God

2ND AND 3RD GRADE

God wants to be your closest friend! He knows everything about you, and wants you to know everything about Him.

The verses below talk about knowing God. Write the word KNOW in the blank spaces.

Psalm 9:10 – "*Those who _____ your name trust in you for you, O lord, do not abandon those who search for you.*"

Psalm 119:168 – "*Yes, I obey your commandments and laws because you _____ everything I do.*"

Psalm 139:23 – "*Search me, O God, and _____ my heart.*"

Daniel 11:32 – "*But the people who _____ their God will be strong and will resist him.*"

John 10:27 – "*My sheep listen to my voice; I _____ them, and they follow me.*"

Phil 3:8 – "*Yes, everything else is worthless when compared with the infinite value of _____ing Christ Jesus my Lord. For his sake, I have discarded everything else, counting it all as garbage, so that I could gain Christ and become one with him.*"

Philippians 3:10 – "*I want to _____ Christ and experience the mighty power that raised him from the dead.*"

Colossians 1:10 – "*You will grow as you learn to _____ God better and better.*"

Bazooka Boys ★ Knowing God

4TH AND 5TH GRADE

God wants to be your closest friend! He knows everything about you, and wants you to know everything about Him.

The verses below talk about knowing God. Look up the scripture and fill in the missing words.

Psalm 9:10 – "Those who _____ your name _____ in you for you, O lord, do not abandon those who search for you."

Psalm 119:168 – "Yes, I obey your commandments and laws because you _____ everything I do."

Psalm 139:23 – "Search me, O God, and _____ my _____."

Daniel 11:32 – "But the people who _____ their God will be _____ and will resist him."

John 10:27 – "My sheep listen to my voice; I _____ them, and they _____ me."

Phil 3:8 – "Yes, everything else is _____ when compared with the infinite value of _____ing Christ Jesus my Lord. For his sake, I have discarded everything else, counting it all as garbage, so that I could gain Christ and become one with him."

Philippians 3:10 – "I want to _____ Christ and experience the mighty _____ that raised him from the dead."

Colossians 1:10 – "You will _____ as you learn to _____ God better and better."

BAZOOKA BLAST OVERVIEW: WEEK 2

Large Group Lesson: *(15 minutes)*

- Overview of the Trinity: God the Father, Jesus, Holy Spirit (water, ice, steam)
- God the Father:
  1. God is our Protector (Psalm 121:7–8)
  2. God is our Provider (Matthew 6:25–27)
  3. God the Father is Perfect: Be sure to address those boys who do not have fathers (*sidebar page 32*)
- **Bazooka Blitz:** Small Group Time:

Bazooka Project *(20 minutes)* Note: Do this project first, you'll use it during the Bible Blitz activity later on in the evening. (Instructions on page 35)

Bible Blitz *(10 minutes)*
God is My Shield *(Instructions on page 37)*

Team Huddle *(10 minutes)*

Ask This:
1. If someone was in danger – how would you protect them?
2. Name one things God provides for your family?
3. Do you know anyone who is perfect?
    Is God perfect?
    How do we know God is perfect?

Repeat This: 1 John 3:1

Pray This: *"God, thanks for being perfect. Thanks for loving me no matter what I do. Thanks for protecting me every day, and thanks for providing for me—that's really cool. Help me to be like You."*

Doodle This: Copy the Doodle page for the boys (or have them turn to the page in their workbooks if they have them)

Take home: Doodle pages, activity sheets and parent connection.

Bazooka Boys ★ Knowing God

GOD THE FATHER

WHAT'S THE POINT?
GOD IS OUR PERFECT HEAVENLY FATHER.
HE LOVES US, PROTECTS US, AND PROVIDES FOR US.

THEME VERSE:

*See how much our Father loves us,
for he calls us his children, and that is what we are!*
1 John 3:1

RELATED BIBLE PASSAGE:

Exodus 16:1–31

★ LARGE GROUP LESSON ★
(15 minutes)

Last week we talked about the fact that God knows everything about you and wants you to know everything about Him. We talked about how we can learn more about God. Who remembers the three ways we can grow closer to God?

1. Read the Bible.
2. Talk to God.
3. Go to Church.

Today we're going to talk some more about what God is like.

There's something about God that is crazy awesome. In fact, it's kind of mind blowing. When you try to think about it, it sometimes makes your brain hurt.

There are three different parts to who God is, yet He is one God. Let me show you what I mean.

> **Trinity Illustration:** The objective is to teach the concept of the Trinity. God is known to us in three persons—God the Father, God and the Son (Jesus), and God the Holy Spirit. Although there are three different parts to Him, they are all God.

Hold up pitcher of water.

    Ask: What is this? (water)

    Answer: This is a pitcher of water. You can drink it on a hot day. You

shower with water so you don't smell bad. You can fill balloons with water and throw them at people.

Hold up ice cubes.

Ask: What are these? (ice cubes)

Answer: These are ice cubes. How do you make ice cubes? You put water in these trays, and then put it in the freezer and it gets really, really cold and then you have ice cubes.

Show them steam.

Ask: What is this? (steam)

Answer: What happens when you boil water? What does water turn into? It turns into steam!

What do all three of these things have in common? They're all water. But they're all different forms of the same thing—water, ice, and steam.

God is the same way! There are three parts to Him. They're all different forms, but they are all the same thing. The same way we have water, ice, steam, we have God the Father, God the Son or Jesus, and God the Holy Spirit. They are one, but different.

Is your brain hurting?

Over the next few weeks, we're going to talk about the three different parts of God—the Father, Son, and Holy Spirit. We're going to learn about each one of them and what makes them different.

Today we're going to start by talking about God the Father.

I think it's really, really cool that God calls himself "Our Father" because fathers are awesome.

Jarred loves to spend time with his Dad. They have a lot in common, especially when it comes to the outdoors. They both love to be outside, go camping, and ride their bikes. Every year, they go to a special camping spot, just the two of them. They set up their tents, build their campfires, and spend a whole week hiking, fishing, and spending time together.

Jarred loves being with his dad. He always knows his dad will make sure he is safe. Even though they go on some crazy adventures, Jarred doesn't worry because his dad is there with him. Even times when Jarred is nervous, he knows his dad is there to keep him safe.

God the Father is the same way with you and me.

 1. GOD IS OUR PROTECTOR

He is always watching over us, protecting us, and keeping us safe from danger and harm. Psalm 121:7–8 explains it in a cool way: *"The Lord keeps you from all harm and watches over your life. The Lord keeps watch over you as you come and go, both now and forever."*

God is always watching over you. In those moments when you feel afraid of something, you can be sure that God is right there with you, keeping you safe.

Bazooka Boys ★ Knowing God

You don't have to be scared or ever, ever, ever feel like you're alone. God is watching over you. He is our protector.

What is a protector? Well, it's like a shield in front of us.

> **Object lesson:** Have someone come to the front and hold up a shield (a garbage can lid, a toy shield, or anything else you can find. They can also wear knee pads, goggles, or anything else you can think of.) Then have some other boys come up and either shoot Nerf guns or throw foam balls or anything else you can think of at the boy who will be safe because the shield protects him.

This shield was a protector! No matter what we threw at him, he was safe because his shield was in front of him making sure that nothing could get to him.

God is your shield! He stands before you and around you and keeps you safe. Psalm 27:1 says, *"The Lord is my light and my salvation—so why should I be afraid? The Lord is my fortress, protecting me from danger, so why should I tremble?"* You don't ever have to be afraid because God is just like a shield, standing in front of you, protecting you from anything that gets thrown at you.

Another great thing about Jarred's camping trips is that his dad makes sure they have everything they'll need. He packs the cooler with food and he catches fish to cook over the fire and eat for dinner. He makes sure he has clothes that are warm enough and shoes that will keep his feet dry. He brings the extra warm sleeping bags for the nights when it gets cold. Jarred never has to worry, because he knows his dad will provide everything he needs.

God the Father is the same way with you and me.

2. GOD IS OUR PROVIDOR

Everything you and I have has been given to us by God the Father. You might think that your parents get you everything you need, but the Bible tells us everything we have comes from God. He provides a job for your mom and dad so they can earn money to buy you things. He makes sure that you have the things you need every single day.

There is a story in Exodus chapter 16 that tells us about God providing for His people. The Israelites were slaves in the nation of Egypt. They had no rights and no freedom. They had to do slave labor all day—whatever the Egyptians told them to do. It was like they were prisoners! One day God used our friend named Moses to lead the Israelites in a huge escape attempt. Even though the Egyptians chased them, God did some cool miracles and all of the Israelites escaped from Egypt. They were free! But now they were in the desert, looking for a new place to live and unfortunately, there was nothing to eat! They were so hungry and wondered what they were going to do.

So they prayed to God and He did something amazing. In the morning, when they got out of their tents and went outside, there was food called "manna" covering the ground. Every morning, they would wake up, look outside, and see food on the ground. God provided food for them every single day!

God is your provider. He provides your food, your clothes, and your house.

Even though He might not give you every single thing you want, He provides everything you need. Sometimes we can worry about things, but it's important to remember that God will always provide for everything we need.

Matthew 6:25–27 says this: *"That is why I tell you not to worry about everyday life—whether you have enough food and drink, or enough clothes to wear. Isn't life more than food, and your body more that clothing? Look at the birds. They don't plant or harvest or store food in barns, for your Heavenly Father feeds them. And aren't you far more valuable to Him than they are? Can all your worries add a single moment to your life?"*

Did you catch that? You know all those birds you can see flying around your house during summer time? The Bible says that God looks after them and makes sure they have a place to live and food to eat. And God cares about you way more than the birds, so of course He is going to make sure you are taken care of. He is our Heavenly Father.

Sometimes our earthly fathers mess up and make mistakes. Sometimes they say things that hurt. Sometimes they have to work and can't be there when we really need them. Some boys grow up not knowing their earthly father because he left a long time ago.

Sometimes dads make mistakes, but not God.

You know what makes God, our Heavenly Father, so awesome?

 ## 3. GOD THE FATHER IS PERFECT

God the Father never makes mistakes. He always does the right thing. He always does what's best for you and He will never, ever leave you.

No matter how much your mom and dad love you, they are still people just like you and me. And people make mistakes. How many of you here have ever made a mistake? How many of you have ever said or done something mean? How many of you have ever done something you wish you could take back? All of us have, because we are humans, and humans are not perfect.

But God is not human. He is God. He never makes mistakes. That makes me feel so safe! I can know that no matter what, God will do the right thing for me every time. I don't ever have to wonder if God forgot about me or if He doesn't love me anymore. He will never let me down. He will never fail me. He will never do anything that isn't perfect.

Just so you know: Some boys don't have a dad in their life. There are lots of reasons this may be the case. You should know that it is never your fault if you don't have a dad who is close to you. It must be really hard sometimes to wish you had a dad like other boys, but you should know that God promises He will be the very best Father you could ever imagine. There's even a verse in the Bible just for you. Psalm 68:5 says, *"A father to the fatherless, a defender of widows, is God in His holy dwelling."* (NIV) You may not have a father here on earth, or maybe you do have a father but you're not close to him. God will step in and be the best father you ever dreamed of having. It's His promise to you.

God is your Heavenly Father. He loves you so much. It's like you're His favorite, and He is so proud of you. Whenever you're scared, imagine your Heavenly Father standing like a shield in front of you. When you're worried about something, remember that He is your Father who will give you everything you need. And when

> "A FATHER TO THE FATHERLESS, A DEFENDER OF WIDOWS, IS GOD IN HIS HOLY DWELLING."
> —PSALM 68:5 (NOV)

Bazooka Boys ★ Knowing God

you need someone to be there for you, you can count always count on God, your Heavenly Father.

Closing Prayer: God, thank you for being my Father. It makes me feel strong and safe knowing You are there with me. Help me to always remember that I am your son, that you love me and are proud of me. Amen.

Bazooka Boys ★ Knowing God

BIBLE SHIELDS

(20 minutes)

Leaders: Make sure you do adequate preparation for the projects, keeping in mind the age and skill level of your group members.

Supplies

- Cardboard
- Scissors
- Crayons/markers
- Duct Tape
- Bible verses
- Rolled up paper for balls (ping pong balls work great too)

Directions

- Cut the cardboard into enough shields for each boy to have one.
- Use the Duct Tape to create a handles on the backs of the shields.
- Have each boy design the front of a shield with markers and Duct Tape.
- Have the boys write the reference of one of the Bible verses, listed in Bazooka Blitz, on the front of their shields.

Bazooka Boys ★ Knowing God

GOD IS MY SHIELD

(10–15 minutes)

Supplies

- Paper balls/ping pong balls
- Bibles
- Shields from the craft project
- Bible references
- Masking tape

Bible Verses

- Matthew 6:25–27
- Psalm 27:1
- Psalm 121:7–8
- 1 John 3:1
- Exodus 16:4

Directions

1. Split the boys into two teams and divide the room in half with one team on each side (divide the room with a line of masking tape).
2. On your mark, have them begin to battle with the paper balls or ping pong balls (Any non-lethal projectile will work). If a boy gets hit with a projectile, they're out.
3. After the battle has raged on for a few minutes, yell "Shields up!" All boys still in the battle must grab their Bibles and look up the Bible verse written on their shield. (You can add more if you like.)
4. The person who finds their reference first can pick a player who is out of the game to come back in. Allow the boys to battle until one team wins.

Bazooka Boys ★ Knowing God

ASK THIS ★ REPEAT THIS ★ PRAY THIS ★ DOODLE THIS
(10 minutes)

Huddle up with your team just before you dismiss.

Ask this:

1. If someone was in danger – how would you protect them?
   Answers: You should get some fun ones!

2. Name one things God provides for your family?
   Possible answer: money, food, clothes, house, job for parents

3. Do you know anyone who is perfect?
   Answer: NO, none of us are perfect.

4. Is God perfect?
   Answer: YES!

5. How do we know God is perfect?
   Possible Answers: He never makes mistakes. He protects us. He provides for us. He loves us.

Repeat This:

   "See how much our Father loves us, for he calls us his children, and that is what we are!" – 1 John 3:1

Pray This:

   "God, thanks for being perfect. Thanks for loving me no matter what I do. Thanks for protecting me every day, and thanks for providing for me—that's really cool. Help me to be like You."

Doodle This:

   Copy the Doodle page for the boys (or have them turn there in their workbooks if they have purchased them).

PARENT CONNECTION

One of the most important things you can give your son is an accurate view of God the Father. It's very easy for them to connect their image of our Heavenly Father with the earthly authorities in their life: their parents, grandparents, teachers, or other people of significance.

First of all, being loving and accepting of them is vital. Many children grow up thinking they aren't good enough. Encourage them every chance you get. Remind them that they are unique and you're proud of them. Even when correcting them, make sure they know you believe in them.

We all know we're imperfect authority figures. Be quick to apologize for moments when you react in anger or are impatient with your kids. Be sure to remind them that, although you are human and will make mistakes, God is perfect and will never fail them. Give them the foundation of His unshakable character and love to stand on.

Bazooka Boys ★ Knowing God

DOODLE PAGE

LESSON 2

Draw as MANY things as you can that God has provided for you and your family!

Bazooka Boys ★ Knowing God

# TAKE HOME ACTIVITY

WEEK 2

KINDERGARDEN AND 1ST GRADE

God is the Best Father EVER! Below there are a list of words that help describe what a great Father God is. Match the word with the spaces provided.

F _____
A _____
T _____
H _____
E _____
R _____

Word List

Fun *Truth* *Everywhere*

Awesome *Holy* *Ready to Listen*

In the verses below, write in the word FATHER in the blank spaces.

Psalm 2:7 – *"The Lord said to me, 'You are my son. Today I have become your _____.'"*

Psalm 89:26 – *"And he will call out to me, "You are my _____, my God, and the Rock of my salvation."'*

Isaiah 9:6 – *"And He will be called: Wonderful Counselor, Mighty God, Everlasting _____, Prince of Peace."*

Matthew 5:16 – *"In the same way, let your good deeds shine out for all to see, so that everyone will praise your heavenly _____."*

Romans 8:15 – *"So you have not received a spirit that makes you fearful slaves. Instead, you received God's Spirit when he adopted you as his own children. Now we call him, 'Abba _____.' For His spirit joins with our spirit to affirm that we are God's children."*

2 Cor 6:18 – *"And I will be your _____, and you will be my sons and daughters, says the Lord Almighty."*

Bazooka Boys ★ Knowing God

TAKE HOME ACTIVITY

2ND AND 3RD GRADE

God is the Best Father EVER! Below there are a list of words that help describe what a great Father God is. Match the word with the spaces provided.

F _____
A _____
T _____
H _____
E _____
R _____

WORD LIST

Fun	*Truth*	*Everywhere*
Awesome	*Holy*	*Ready to Listen*

In the verses below, write in the word FATHER in the blank spaces.

Psalm 2:7 – *"The Lord said to me, 'You are my son. Today I have become your _____.'"*

Psalm 89:26 – *"And he will call out to me, "You are my _____, my God, and the Rock of my salvation."'*

Isaiah 9:6 – *"And He will be called: Wonderful Counselor, Mighty God, Everlasting _____, Prince of Peace."*

Matthew 5:16 – *"In the same way, let your good deeds shine out for all to see, so that everyone will praise your heavenly _____."*

Romans 8:15 – *"So you have not received a spirit that makes you fearful slaves. Instead, you received God's Spirit when he adopted you as his own children. Now we call him, 'Abba _____.' For His spirit joins with our spirit to affirm that we are God's children."*

2 Cor 6:18 – *"And I will be your _____, and you will be my sons and daughters, says the Lord Almighty."*

Bazooka Boys ★ Knowing God

4ᵀᴴ AND 5ᵀᴴ GRADE

God is the Best Father EVER! Write words that describe God the Father that begin with each letter provided below.

F _____

A _____

T _____

H _____

E _____

R _____

WORD LIST

Fun	*Truth*	*Everywhere*
Awesome	*Holy*	*Ready to Listen*

Look up the verses below, write in the missing words in the blank spaces.

Psalm 2:7 – "*The Lord said to me, 'You are my son. Today I have become your _____.'*"

Psalm 89:26 – "*And he will call out to me, "You are my _____, my God, and the _____ of my salvation."*"

Isaiah 9:6 – "*And He will be called: Wonderful _____, Mighty God, Everlasting _____, Prince of Peace.*"

Matthew 5:16 – "*In the same way, let your good _____ shine out for all to see, so that everyone will praise your heavenly _____.*"

Romans 8:15 – "*So you have not received a spirit that makes you fearful _____. Instead, you received God's Spirit when he adopted you as his own _____. Now we call him, 'Abba _____.' For His spirit joins with our spirit to affirm that we are God's children.*"

2 Cor 6:18 – "*And I will be your _____, and you will be my sons and _____, says the Lord Almighty.*"

Bazooka Boys ★ Knowing God

WEEK 2

BAZOOKA BLAST OVERVIEW: WEEK 3

Large Group Lesson: *(15 minutes)*

- All of us were born with a sinful nature which separated us from God. (Romans 3:23)
- Jesus came to Earth and died on the cross to make a way for us to have access to God. (John 3:16)
- Because of what Jesus did for us, we can have a close relationship with God.

Bazooka Blitz: Small Group Time:

Bible Blitz *(15 minutes)*
Paper Plane Toss *(Instructions on page 57)*

Bazooka Project *(20 minutes)*
Duct Tape All Access Lanyard *(Instructions on page 59)*

Team Huddle *(10 minutes)*

Ask This:

1. If you could have an all access pass to meet anyone, who would it be?

2. How can we get an all access pass to God?

3. Why did God send His only son, Jesus, to die for us?

Repeat This: Romans 5:11

Pray This: *"God, thanks for sending Your son Jesus to die for me. Even though it was hard, I know you did it because You love me and wanted to give me an all access pass to You. Thanks for loving me no matter what. I love You and give my life to You. Help me be Your friend."*

Doodle This: *(Follow Doodle page instructions)*

Take home: Doodle pages, activity sheets and parent connection.

Bazooka Boys ★ Knowing God

GOD THE SON (JESUS)

WHAT'S THE POINT?
JESUS CAME TO EARTH AND DIED ON THE CROSS
TO GIVE US AN ALL ACCESS PASS TO GOD.

THEME VERSE:
So now we can rejoice in our wonderful new relationship with God because our Lord Jesus Christ has made us friends of God.
Romans 5:11

RELATED BIBLE PASSAGE:
Genesis 3

★ LARGE GROUP LESSON ★
(15 minutes)

Last week we learned about God as our Heavenly Father. There were three things we said about God the Father. Do you remember what they were?

1. He protects us.
2. He provides for us.
3. He is perfect.

Today we are going to talk about God the Son, who is Jesus.

Jesus is God's Son. He was in heaven with the Father and the Holy Spirit, but there was a problem with people on the earth that God had created. How many of you have heard the story of Adam and Eve?

Adam and Eve were the first people God ever created. Genesis 1 tells us about God creating man and woman and giving them one rule. They were not supposed to eat the fruit from a certain tree in the garden. But Adam and Eve did not follow the rules that God gave them, and the moment that they disobeyed God, sin entered the world. Sin is not just the things you and I do that are wrong—sin became part of who we are.

> **Example:** How many of you have little brothers or sisters? Have heard them say "Mine!" and get kind of mean? Have you had them hit you or be selfish? Who taught them to be naughty? Did you teach your little sister to be mean? Did your mom and dad sit them down and tell them that they should scream and cry when they don't get their own way? No! They were just born that way. You and I were too.

Each and every one of us was born with a sinful nature. The Bible tells us in Romans 3:23: *"For everyone has sinned; we all fall short of God's glorious standard."* Every one of us makes mistakes, does the wrong thing, and thinks only about ourselves. It doesn't mean that we're bad, it just means that we're born imperfect. We're born with a sinful nature.

"FOR GOD LOVED THE WORLD SO MUCH THAT HE GAVE HIS ONE AND ONLY SON, SO THAT EVERYONE WHO BELIEVES IN HIM WILL NOT PERISH BUT HAVE ETERNAL LIFE." —JOHN 3:16

But God is perfect. He doesn't have a sinful nature like you and me. He never does the wrong thing. He has never sinned. He is perfect. And because He is perfect and holy, He cannot be around sin. He just can't.

God loves us so much that He wanted to find a way to be close to us even though our nature is sinful. This is where Jesus comes in. John 3:16 says, *"For God loved the world so much that He gave His one and only son, so that everyone who believes in Him will not perish but have eternal life."*

Jesus is God's son. He is perfect and sinless just like God the Father. So God came up with a plan. Jesus would come down to earth as a person just like you and me. He would be fully God and yet fully human. And He would live a perfect life without sinning at all. Who knows how Jesus came to earth? What holiday celebrates when Jesus

came down to earth? That's right—Christmas! Jesus came down to earth as a little baby who was born in a stable and laid in a manger on Christmas!

Jesus came to earth for a very important reason. The only way God could be close to us was if Jesus died on the cross and rose again. If He did that, there would be a way for us to have a close relationship with God even though we're sinful people. So that's exactly what Jesus did.

Jesus came to earth, grew up and became a man, and lived a sinless life. When He was 33 years old, He died on the cross. But three days after He died, He rose again! And then He went back up to heaven to be with the Father once again.

When He did that, something amazing happened—now we have a way to be close to God. Even though we're sinful people, you and I can have a relationship with God because of what Jesus did on the cross! Isn't that awesome?

There was a boy named Cameron who went to see his favorite football team play a championship game. Not only was this his favorite team, but his favorite

quarterback in the whole world was playing in this game. He couldn't believe he was going to get to see him play in person!

After the game was over, he noticed people walking through a door that said "Locker Room Access." He wondered what was back there and so he walked closer to get a better look. On the other side of the door, he saw the quarterback—his favorite quarterback— standing outside the locker room! Cameron could hardly believe what he was seeing. He saw other people walking

through the door, so he walked over, crazy excited that he was going to get the chance to meet his favorite player.

But the security guard at the door stopped him and said, "I'm sorry, but you can't go back there without one of these." He held up a lanyard that had a little card on the bottom that said "All Access." He was so disappointed. He knew that his absolute favorite, favorite, favorite football player was right behind that door and if he could just get through, he would be able to meet him and get to know him and spend time with him. But he couldn't get through that door without the all access pass.

Then all of the sudden, a coach walked up beside him and smiled. He held up something in his hand. Cameron could hardly believe it—it was an all access pass. The nice man looked at him and

> SO NOW WE CAN REJOICE IN OUR WONDERFUL NEW RELATIONSHIP WITH GOD BECAUSE OUR LORD JESUS CHRIST HAS MADE US FRIENDS OF GOD.
> —ROMANS 5:11

said, "Would you like to have this?"

Would he like to have this pass? Are you kidding me? Of course he wanted the pass! Like crazy! With that pass he could spend time with the most amazingly awesome person in the universe!

He could hardly get the words out of his mouth. "Yes! I would love it! Thank you so much!" The coach placed the lanyard around his neck and Cameron walked through the door and got to meet his favorite football player.

That's exactly what Jesus did for you and me. We were separated from God. We couldn't be close to Him because of our sinful nature. There was a big door between us and Him. But when

Jesus came to earth and died on the cross, He made a way for you and me to have an all access pass to God. We can have a relationship with Him. We can know Him. We can be close to Him. Through Jesus, we can be forgiven of all our sins!

So how do you get that all access pass to God? Simply ask Jesus for it! Ask Him to come into your life and forgive you for all the things you've done wrong. Ask Him to come and live in your heart. When you ask Jesus into your life, He places a big all access pass around your neck. You're forgiven of your sins and can have a close, personal relationship with God. Romans 5:11 says, *"So now we can rejoice in our wonderful new relationship with God because our Lord Jesus Christ has made us friends of God."*

The whole reason Jesus came to earth and died for you and me was simply that He loved us so very much. He wanted to be close to you, so He provided a way to make it happen. Aren't you thankful Jesus died on the cross for you?

Maybe some of you have never asked Jesus to come into your hearts and you want to ask Him to forgive you of your sins and put a big all access pass around your neck. Today you can invite Jesus into your life and begin living your life in a close, personal relationship with Him.

Everyone, please bow your heads and close your eyes. Jesus would love to have a relationship with you. He died on the cross because He loved you so much and today you can ask Him to come into your heart. If you would like to do that, please raise your hand and then we can pray together.

Closing Prayer: Pray this prayer with me: "Dear Jesus, thank You for coming to earth and dying on the cross. Please forgive me for all my sins and come into my life. I want to live for You, and I want to spend time getting to know You more so I can be closer to You. Thank You for coming into my heart. Amen."

PAPER PLANE TOSS

(15 minutes)

Supplies

- Paper
- Pen
- Bible references
- Bibles
- Measuring Tape

Directions

1. Write each Bible reference on a separate piece of paper (you can add more if you like).
   - Romans 5:11
   - John 3:16
   - Romans 3:23
   - John 14:3
   - John 14:6
   - Romans 6:23
   - Romans 10:9–10
   - Genesis 3:4–5

2. Give each boy one piece of paper with a Scripture reference on it.

3. Challenge them to create the paper airplane that will fly the farthest distance. (Some boys will need your help crafting their airplane, so be sure you know how to fold several types of paper airplanes. Google and YouTube are your friends.)

4. When the boys are finished, split them up into two teams. (If you don't have enough boys for team competition, individual competition is always good. Be sure to give the younger boys a little advantage over the older boys.)

5. Have one boy from each team stand at a designated throwing line. On your mark, have each boy throw their plane. Measure and mark the distance of each plane. The plane that has gone the farthest wins the round.

6. Take the winning plane and open it up. Have one boy from the winning team look up the Scripture reference. Once he reads it, ask someone to explain what they think it means.

7. Repeat the process until all the verses have been read. Here's an idea: keep track of the boy who flew his plane the farthest and recognize him. Boys love to be recognized for their accomplishments.

DUCT TAPE ALL ACCESS LANYARD

(20 minutes)

Supplies

- Duct tape (three feet for each boy)
- Scissors
- Key rings
- Sharpie markers
- Laynard hooks (optional)
- Cardstock (optional)
- Single hole punch

Directions

1. Give each boy three feet of duct tape

2. Fold the duct tape in half the long way, sticky sides together. (Hint: Do it slowly—once the two sticky sides touch, there's no pulling them apart. It might be easier to work with three 12" pieces, overlapping the ends.

3. Make a loop by putting the two ends through your key ring (you can put it around your neck if that would be easier).

4. Fold the pieces over the key ring and tape them to the straps (2 inch x 1 inch strip of tape).

5. If needed, secure the straps with another piece of tape.

6. Write "All Access Pass" down the length of the duct tape

7. Optional:
    - Attach a lanyard hook to the key ring
    - Cut a 3" x 4" piece of cardstock

- Cover both sides of the cardstock with duct tape and trim off excess tape
- Punch a hole in the middle of the top of the cardstock
- Attach the cardstock to the lanyard hook
- Write "All Access Pass" on the cardstock

ASK THIS ★ REPEAT THIS ★ PRAY THIS ★ DOODLE THIS
(10 minutes)

Huddle up with your team just before you dismiss.

Ask this

1. If you could have an all access pass to meet anyone, who would it be?"

2. How can we get an all access pass to God?"
   Answer: By believing in Jesus and giving our lives to Him.

3. Why did God send His only son, Jesus, to die for us?"
   Answer: Because He loved us and wanted to have a close relationship with us.

Repeat this:

So now we can rejoice in our wonderful new relationship with God because our Lord Jesus Christ has made us friends of God." – Romans 5:11

Pray this:

"God, thanks for sending Your son Jesus to die for me. Even though it was hard, I know you did it because You love me and wanted to give me an all access pass to You. Thanks for loving me no matter what. I love You and give my life to You. Help me be Your friend."

Doodle this:

Copy the Doodle page for the boys (or have them turn in their workbooks if they have purchased them)

PARENT CONNECTION

This week in Bazooka Boys, we talked about our need for Jesus to make a way for us to have a relationship with God. We started by discussing the Fall of Man in Genesis, where Adam and Eve disobeyed God. Because of their sin, we're all born with a sinful nature. We shared that each and every one of us is separated from God because He's sinless and perfect, and we're all sinful people. God wanted to have a relationship with us, so He needed to make a way for us to be forgiven for our sins.

He sent Jesus to the earth to live a sinless life, die on the cross, and then come back to life. His amazing sacrifice provided a way for us to be back in close relationship with God. Jesus' work on the cross provided us with a way to have "all access" to God. We simply need to ask Jesus to come into our lives and forgive us of our sins, and we'll be saved. Once we ask Jesus into our hearts, we're clean and forgiven and can have a relationship with God!

We gave the boys the opportunity to ask Jesus into their hearts! This is a great time to ask your son about his relationship with Jesus and if he has asked Jesus into his life. This is the beginning of his personal relationship with God and it's important to nurture and grow his faith.

When he is apprehensive or upset, remind him that Jesus lives in his heart now, and so he is never, ever alone. When he doesn't know what to do in a situation, tell him Jesus is very close to him and will speak to his heart about how he should handle a problem. Emphasize that he has a personal connection with Jesus and can talk to Him anytime.

Bazooka Boys ★ Knowing God

DOODLE PAGE

LESSON 3

"When Jesus came to earth and died on the cross, He made a way for us to be close to God. Draw a bridge that symbolized what Jesus did for us.

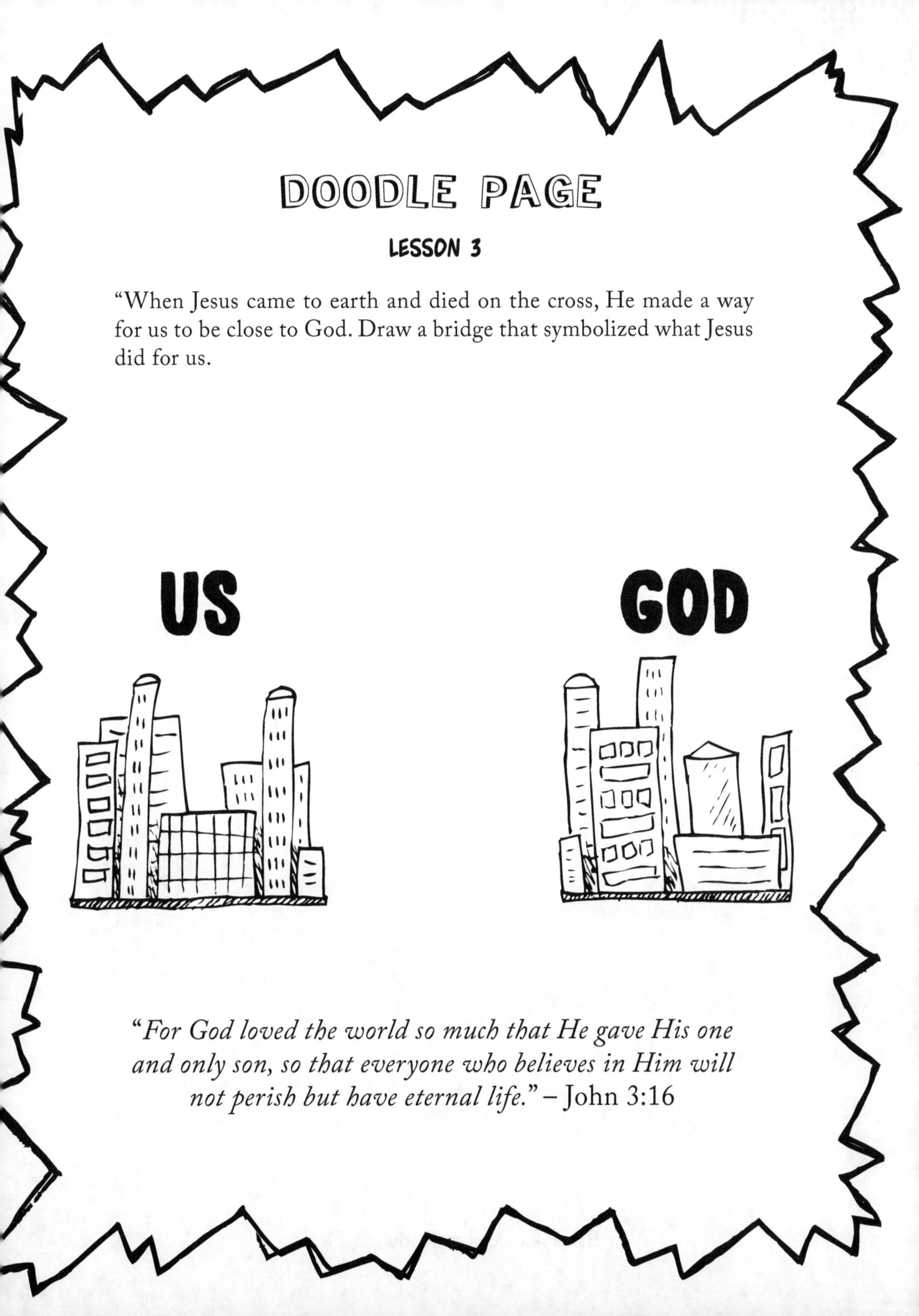

"For God loved the world so much that He gave His one and only son, so that everyone who believes in Him will not perish but have eternal life." – John 3:16

Bazooka Boys ★ Knowing God

TAKE HOME ACTIVITY

KINDERGARDEN AND 1ST GRADE

In your Bible, look up Romans 5:8. Write out the verse here.

WEEK 3

Bazooka Boys ★ Knowing God

2ND AND 3RD GRADE

Romans 5 talks about how sin entered the world through the sin of Adam, and how Jesus coming provided a way for us to be forgiven of our sins. Read through Romans 5 in your Bible, and write out the following verses below.

Romans 5:12: _____
_____
_____.

Romans 5:15 _____
_____
_____.

Romans 5:16 _____
_____
_____.

Romans 5:17 _____
_____
_____.

Romans 5:18 _____
_____
_____.

Bazooka Boys ★ Knowing God

4TH AND 5TH GRADE

Romans 5 talks about how sin entered the world through the sin of Adam, and how Jesus coming provided a way for us to be forgiven of our sins. Read through Romans 5 in your Bible, and write out the following verses below.

Romans 5:12: _____
_____
_____.

Romans 5:15 _____
_____
_____.

Romans 5:16 _____
_____
_____.

Romans 5:17 _____
_____
_____.

Romans 5:18 _____
_____
_____.

Now write out a prayer thanking God for His salvation and what He did for us on the cross:

_____
_____
_____
_____
_____
_____
_____
_____
_____
_____
_____
_____
_____
_____.

Bazooka Boys ★ Knowing God

WEEK 3

Large Group Lesson: *(15 minutes)*

When Jesus left earth and went back to heaven, He sent us the Holy Spirit to speak to us and show us all the things we need to know. (John 15:26)

- The Holy Spirit makes us strong (Acts 1:8)
- The Holy Spirit is our teacher (John 14:26)
- The Holy Spirit is our guide (Psalm 143:10)

Bazooka Blitz: Small Group Time:

    Bible Blitz *(15 minutes)*
        Pyramid Smash *(Instructions on page 81)*
    Bazooka Project *(20 minutes)*
        Magnetic Compass Project *(Instructions on page 83)*
    Team Huddle *(10 minutes)*

    <u>Ask This:</u>

    1. Who's the strongest person you know? What makes him strong?

    2. The Holy Spirit makes us strong. Name one area of your life where you want to be stronger.

    3. How can the Holy Spirit help you everyday?
        Possible answers: He makes us strong; He teaches us; He guides us.

    <u>Repeat This:</u> John 14:16

    <u>Pray This:</u> *"Thank you, God, for sending your Spirit to earth to help me every day. Help me be strong. Teach me all about You and show me how to live a good life."*

    <u>Doodle This:</u> *(Doodle page instructions on page 87)*

    <u>Take home:</u> Doodle pages, activity sheets and parent connection.

GOD THE HOLY SPIRIT

What's the Point?
Jesus sent us the Holy Spirit to give us power and be our teacher and guide.

THEME VERSE

Then I will ask the Father to send you the Holy Spirit who will help you and always be with you.
John 14:16 (CEV)

RELATED BIBLE STORY

Acts 2:1–4

★ LARGE GROUP LESSON ★
(15 minutes)

How many of you have ever played tag? You chase everyone around the room, and when you finally touch someone, what do you say? "Tag—you're it!"

Last week we talked about Jesus coming to earth and dying on the cross to make a way for us have an all access pass to God. When Jesus lived on earth, He picked twelve people called the disciples to be His friends and travel around with Him while He taught them all the things they needed to know about God.

But after Jesus rose from the dead, He told the disciples He was going to leave. He was going back to heaven. John 16:5 says, "But now I am going away to the one who sent me." Can you imagine how the disciples must have felt?

How many of you have had a really good friend move away? Someone you loved hanging out with and spending time together? When they told you they were leaving, how did you feel? You probably felt bummed and disappointed and sad and lots of other things.

The disciples felt the same way when Jesus told them He was leaving earth and going back to heaven, but then Jesus told them something else really amazing. He said that He had to go away, but He was going to send someone back to earth to be here with us forever. Do you know who that is? The Holy Spirit.

Bazooka Boys ★ Knowing God

Jesus had to leave, but when He left he said "Tag—you're it!" to the Holy Spirit! Now it's the Holy Spirit's job to teach us and speak to us and show us all the things we need to know.

John 15:26 says, *"I will send you the Spirit who comes from the Father and shows what is true. The Spirit will help you and will tell you about me"* (CEV).

So Jesus went back up into heaven and a few days later, the Holy Sprit came down to the disciples. Now, instead of Jesus teaching them all the things about God and helping them know what to do, the Holy Spirit would speak to them and guide them. And He is still here and will speak to you and me to help us know God better!

The big difference is that the Holy Spirit doesn't have a human body like Jesus did. You can't see Him. You can't hear His voice with your ears like you can hear

your teachers at school telling you things, but you can hear Him speak in your heart. Sometimes you will just have a gut feeling, and that's the Holy Spirit speaking to you. We can't see Him with our eyes, but He is always with us.

The Bible talks about a few specific things the Holy Spirit does.

First, the Holy Spirit...

 ## 1. MAKE US STRONG

Who is the most powerful person you can think of? Superman? A professional wrestler? A football player? Being powerful means you're not only strong, but you know how to use your strength in the best way possible.

Acts 1:8 says, *"But you will receive power when the Holy Spirit comes upon you."* When the Holy Spirit comes and lives in our lives, it gives us the power to stand up for what's right. It gives us the courage to tell others about Jesus. It makes us strong and able to do great things for God.

I don't know about you, but I want to be as strong as I can possibly be! Sometimes I don't feel very strong. Sometimes I'm afraid or feel nervous about things. But you know what? Whenever you're scared or nervous or sad, the Holy Spirit will help you. He is with you wherever you go—all the time! Say a prayer and ask Him to help you feel brave and strong, and He will help you get through whatever it is you're facing.

The second thing the Holy Spirit does is promise to...

 ## 2. BE YOUR TEACHER

Jackson loves his teacher, Mr. Crenshaw. He's the best teacher ever and shows Jackson how to do all kinds of really cool things and helps

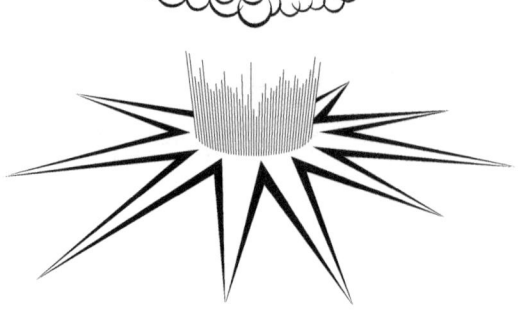

Bazooka Boys ★ Knowing God

him understand stuff that is hard to understand. He's patient and always willing to listen whenever Jackson has a question. He's really encouraging and always tells Jackson he's doing a good job.

But Mr. Crenshaw helps Jackson in another way. Whenever Jackson has a spelling test, he hands it in to Mr. Crenshaw, who takes out a big red marker and circles all the words he got wrong. When Jackson sees the big red marks, he knows what he needs to work on and the things he needs to try harder at.

"THE COMPANION, THE HOLY SPIRIT, WHOM THE FATHER WILL SEND IN MY NAME, WILL TEACH YOU EVERYTHING AND WILL REMIND YOU OF EVERYTHING I TOLD YOU."
—JOHN 14:26 (CEB)

The Holy Spirit is a great teacher, too. He'll show you all kinds of things about God. He'll help you understand the Bible. He'll help you know what Jesus wants you to do and show you how to live a life that makes God the Father happy. John 14:26 says, *"The Companion, the Holy Spirit, whom the Father will send in my name, will teach you everything and will remind you of everything I told you."* (CEB)

The Holy Spirit will also help you know when you've done something wrong. How many of you have ever made a mistake or done something wrong and all of the sudden you get a feeling in your gut that makes you feel really bad about what you did? That's the Holy Spirit! He'll draw big red circles around the things in your life that you need to change and areas of your behavior or attitude that don't make God happy. He shows us these things so we can learn to do better and make the right choices.

The last thing the Holy Spirit does is . . .

3. GUIDE YOU

Have you ever been lost? Have you ever looked around and realized you didn't know which way to go? Sometimes it's easy for us to get lost in our lives. We don't know what we should do, but the Holy Spirit promises to guide us!

Joshua had a big decision to make. He had been asked to join the traveling baseball team for the summer, but if he joined the team, he knew he would miss out on a lot of other activities he wanted to be part of. He couldn't decide what to do! His mom and dad told him he needed to make his own decision, but Joshua was torn. Although he loved playing baseball, he was also interested in going to summer camp and taking drum lessons and even spending some extra time with his little brother. He needed help to know what to do.

So Joshua prayed. He asked God to help him make the decision. One morning he woke up, and in his gut, he knew what his decision should be. It was so crazy! Nothing in particular happened, he just knew that he should pass on baseball this year and spend time doing other things. It just felt like the right thing.

What changed? How did Joshua know what to do? The Holy Spirit guided him in making the right decision. When he prayed, he was asking for the Holy Spirit's help, and He gave Joshua the answer he was looking for.

Bazooka Boys ★ Knowing God

If you don't know what to do in a situation, why not stop and ask the Holy Spirit to guide you? Maybe you're not sure if you should say something. Ask the Holy Spirit if you should speak up or stay quiet. Maybe you're wondering if you should do something your friends are doing. The Holy Spirit will speak to you and help you know what the right thing is, and He'll give you the courage to do the right thing too!

Psalm 143:10 says, *"Teach me to do your will, for you are my God. May your gracious Spirit lead me forward on a firm footing."* God will guide you. The Holy Spirit will speak to you and help you know where to go, what to say, and how to act.

Aren't you glad that Jesus sent us the Holy Spirit? I'm so thankful that when Jesus left, He didn't leave us all on earth alone with no one to show what to do. I'm glad he "tagged" the Holy Spirit to come down to earth to make us strong, be our teacher, and guide us.

Closing Prayer: Dear God, Thank You for sending the Holy Spirit to help me. Thank you that I can know He will make me stronger, teach me things about You, and guide me into making the right choices in my life. Help me to know His voice. Amen.

Bazooka Boys ★ Knowing God

PYRAMID SMASH

(15 minutes)

<u>Supplies</u>

- Styrofoam cups
- Bible references
- Tape (or tennis ball or raquet ball)
- Bibles
- Marker

<u>Bible References</u>

- John 14:16
- Acts 2:1–4
- John 15:26
- Acts 1:8
- John 14:26
- Psalms 143:10

<u>Directions</u>

1. Write the Scripture references on the cups.

2. Break the boys into two teams.

3. Stack two pyramids of 20 styrofoam cups each a good throwing distance from the cups.

4. Make two balls using the tape (a tennis ball or racquetball works well too).

5. Each team should line up behind a designated starting line. On your command, have a boy from each team throw their balls at their team's pyramid.

6. Once the boys hit their pyramid, they can run to it, grab a cup, and look up the Scripture verse written on it. The person who finds the reference first is the winner. The team that hit their pyramid first may not be the winner. Keep track of who wins each round. Play until one team wins.

MAGNETIC COMPASS PROJECT

(To be done as a group – 20 minutes)

Say this: "The Holy Spirit guide us like a compass. Let's make our own compass to see how it works."

Supplies:

- Bowl of water
- Sewing pin or needle
- Magnet
- Small piece of craft foam, cork or paper.

Directions:

1. Cut a small circle from the craft foam, cork or paper.
2. Turn the sewing needle into a magnet by stroking the needle across the magnet about thirty to forty times. Be sure to stroke in one direction only. Not back and forth. The needle will then be magnetized.
3. Place the needle on to the circle cut from your chosen material.
4. Place the circle in the middle of a bowl of water away from the edge of the bowl.
5. The needle will begin to slowly turn around and eventually it will point North and South.
6. Check the accuracy with an actual compass or compass app.

Say this: "Every magnet has a north and south pole. A compass is a small magnet that aligns itself with the north and south poles of the Earth's magnetic field. As the needle is stroked across the magnet, it becomes magnetized because the electrons within the needle straighten up and align themselves with the magnet. The magnetized needle then aligns itself with the Earth's magnetic field when it is placed on top of the water. If you don't know what to do in a situation, why not stop and ask the Holy Spirit to guide you? "

Bazooka Boys ★ Knowing God

ASK THIS ★ REPEAT THIS ★ PRAY THIS ★ DOODLE THIS
(10 minutes)

Huddle up with your team just before you dismiss.

Ask This

1. Who's the strongest person you know? What makes him strong?

2. The Holy Spirit makes us strong. Name one area of your life where you want to be stronger.

3. How can the Holy Spirit help you everyday?
   Possible answers: He makes us strong; He teaches us; He guides us.

Repeat This:

"Then I will ask the Father to send you the Holy Spirit who will help you and always be with you." – John 14:16 (CEV)

Pray this:

"Thank you, God, for sending your Spirit to earth to help me every day. Help me be strong. Teach me all about You and show me how to live a good life."

Doodle this:

Copy the Doodle page for the boys (or have them turn in their workbooks if they have purchased them)

PARENT CONNECTION

This week in Bazooka Boys, your son learned about the Holy Spirit. When Jesus went back into heaven after the resurrection, He promised He would not leave us alone on the earth but would send the Holy Spirit to be with us.

The Holy Spirit's role in our lives is so important. There are countless ways He speaks wisdom and discernment to our hearts, but today we focused on three main attributes of the Holy Spirit.

First off, the Holy Spirit makes us strong. He gives us the power to do the right thing and stand up for what's right. When your son is scared, or sad, or lonely, remind him that the Holy Spirit is with him and has promised to make him brave. He can know that he's never alone and that the Holy Spirit will bring him courage.

The Holy Spirit is also our teacher. He will help us learn and understand the Bible. He'll help us know God better, and He'll help us know right from wrong. The Holy Spirit will speak to our hearts when we've done something that isn't pleasing to God so we can stop our behavior and make the right choice.

Lastly, we learned that the Holy Spirit is our guide. He will help us make decisions and choose the right path for our lives. Encourage your son to pray about decisions and listen for the voice of the Holy Spirit giving him direction. Affirm that he can ask for direction and God will help him know what choices to make. The more independence he gets, the more he'll need to rely on the guidance of the Holy Spirit, so nurturing and developing this part of his spiritual walk is important at his young age.

Bazooka Boys ★ Knowing God

Bazooka Boys ★ Knowing God

TAKE HOME ACTIVITY

KINDERGARDEN AND 1ST GRADE

Solve the puzzle by substituting the numbers for the letters.

1	2	3	4	5	6	7	8	9	10	11	12	13	14	15
A	Q	I	P	F	V	X	N	Y	D	W	Z	K	S	G

16	17	18	19	20	21	22	23	24	25	26
O	U	R	C	E	M	H	T	L	J	B

___ _____ _____ _____
 3   11 3 24 24   1 14 13   23 22 20

_____.   _____   _____
 5 1 23 22 20 18   1 8 10   22 20

_____   _____   _____
11 3 24 24   15 3 6 20   9 16 17

_____   _____
1 8 16 23 22 20 18   5 18 3 20 8 10

_____   _____   _____   _____
23 16   22 20 24 4   9 16 17   1 8 10

_____   _____   _____   _____
23 16   26 20   11 3 23 22   9 16 17

                                                    14:16 NIV

_____.   _____
5 16 18 20 6 20 18   25 16 22 8

Bazooka Boys ★ Knowing God

TAKE HOME ACTIVITY

2ND AND 3RD GRADE

Look up each scripture in the Bible and fill in the blank. (The words are listed below.)

But you will receive _____ when the Holy Spirit comes on you; and you will be my witnesses in Jerusalem, and in Judea and Samaria, and to the ends of the earth. – Acts 1:8 (NIV)

³Give _____ to the God and Father of our Lord Jesus Christ! He is the Father who gives tender love. All comfort comes from him. ⁴He _____ us in all our troubles. Now we can comfort others when they are in trouble. We ourselves have received comfort from God. – 2 Corinthians 1:3-4 (CEV)

I will send the _____ to you from the Father. He is the Spirit of truth, who comes out from the Father. When the Friend comes to _____ you, he will give witness about me. – John 15:26 (CEV)

I baptize you with water, but he will baptize you with the _____. – Mark 1:8 (NIV)

The angel answered, 'The Holy Spirit will come on you, and the _____ of the Most High will overshadow you. So the holy one to be born will be called the Son of God'. – Luke 1:35 (NIV)

WORD LIST

power   *thanks*   *Holy Spirit*
help   *power*
Holy Spirit   *comforts*

Bazooka Boys ★ Knowing God

4TH AND 5TH GRADE

Look up each scripture in the Bible and fill in the blank (the words are listed below).

But you will receive _____ when the Holy Spirit comes on you; and you will be my witnesses in Jerusalem, and in Judea and Samaria, and to the ends of the earth. – Acts 1:8 (NIV)

³Give _____ to the God and Father of our Lord Jesus Christ! He is the Father who gives tender love. All comfort comes from him. ⁴He _____ us in all our troubles. Now we can comfort others when they are in trouble. We ourselves have received comfort from God. – 2 Corinthians 1:3-4 (CEV)

I will send the _____ to you from the Father. He is the Spirit of truth, who comes out from the Father. When the Friend comes to _____ you, he will give witness about me. – John 15:26 (CEV)

I baptize you with water, but he will baptize you with the _____. – Mark 1:8 (NIV)

The angel answered, 'The Holy Spirit will come on you, and the _____ of the Most High will overshadow you. So the holy one to be born will be called the Son of God'. – Luke 1:35 (NIV)

May the God of hope fill you with all _____ and _____ as you trust in him, so that you may overflow with hope by the power of the Holy Spirit. – Romans 15:13 (NIV)

But the _____ of the Spirit is love, joy, peace, forbearance, kindness, goodness, faithfulness, gentleness and self-control. Against such things there is no law. – Galatians 5:22, 23 (NIV)

You _____ me with your counsel. – Psalm 73:24 (NIV)

But the _____, the Holy Spirit, whom the Father will send in my name, will _____ you all things and will remind you of everything I have said to you. – John 14:26 (NIV)

¹⁰ Just as Jesus was coming up out of the _____, he saw heaven being torn open and the _____ descending on him like a dove. ¹¹ And a voice came from heaven: "You are my _____, whom I love; with you I am well pleased. – Mark 1:10, 11 (NIV)

Word List

Holy Spirit	*Holy Spirit*	*water*
Son	*thanks*	*comforts*
advocate	*teach*	*fruit*
power	*power*	*joy*
peace	*guide*	*help*

Bazooka Boys ★ Knowing God

KNOWING GOD

WEEK 5

BAZOOKA BASH

The Bazooka Bash is a night for your boys to connect, invite their friends, and have FUN! Put together an exciting, rocking party for the boys to simply enjoy each other. Plan some fun activities, and tell their friends how FUN it is to be in Bazooka Boys! This is a great way to give the boys something awesome to look forward to and when they're excited about something – they tell their friends! Really encourage them to bring a friend from school or their neighborhood with them.

There is no "lesson" for this night, because we simply want the boys to connect. I promise you, if their friends have an amazing night – they will want to come back! This is a great way to introduce the boys in your community to your church and leaders. Make sure your event is AWESOME!

At the end of the evening, be sure to send invited friends a promotional piece about your ministry. Invite them back to your church for the weekend or to a special event with their parents!

Bazooka Boys Theme: Motorcycle Party!

Food: Pizza, Chips and Candy!

Décor & Giveaways:

- How about giving each boy a bandanna to tie around their head! Get some dollar store sunglasses and make your guys look ultra cool.
- No biker is complete without some tattoos! Set up a tattoo station and let the boys have fun with temporary tattoos.
- Decorate with orange, black and red. Use "leather looking" fabrics on the tables.

Games & Activities:

- Contact your local Motorcycle store or members of your church who own bikes. Ask them to bring some awesome motorcycles to the church. Take pictures of the boys on the motorcycles!
- "Motorcycle" races
    a. Set up a track or course and let the boys race each other... on TRICYCLES! Make them go around cones and create a finish line for them to race through!
- Consider renting games or inflatables
    b. Bouncy Houses
    c. Golf zones
    d. Laser tag
    e. Inflatable Sumo wrestling Suits
    f. Inflatable Jousting Competition
- Musical Chair! This is a great friendship building game. It is a version of Musical Chairs with a difference. Instead of removing a player and a chair from the game each time the music stops, only remove a chair! This eventually means that the group will end up having to squeeze onto one chair. Make sure the chairs you are using are sturdy because even the strongest chair will struggle under the weight of many boys!

Bazooka Boys ★ Knowing God

- Silent Interview (Similar to charades)
    1. Split the group up into pairs and have each pair tell each other three things about themselves - but without speaking.
    2. When they have had enough time to trying to figure out what their partner was trying to convey, bring everyone back into the group and have each person introduce their partner, and the things they think they learned about them. This game can reveal interesting facts about each person and helps to build bonds between friends.
- Tower of Mallow
    1. Give each small group several packets of both marshmallows and dry spaghetti.
    2. Tell them to build a marshmallow tower as high as they can.
    3. The tower has to be able to withstand its own weight, and the tallest wins a prize.

This game is perfect to teach boys of all ages about teamwork, cooperation, friendship and coordination. It also helps foster new friendships among boys who haven't played together before.

Bazooka Boys ★ Knowing God

BAZOOKA BASH PARTY!

BAZOOKA BASH PARTY!

BAZOOKA BASH PARTY!

Come for a fun night to hang out with the boys and do cool activities, awesome games, and have snacks! Bring a friend!

Where _____

When _____

BAZOOKA BASH PARTY!

Come for a fun night to hang out with the boys and do cool activities, awesome games, and have snacks! Bring a friend!

Where _____

When _____

www.ingramcontent.com/pod-product-compliance
Lightning Source LLC
Chambersburg PA
CBHW060516300426
44112CB00017B/2697